Ryan

by Iain Gray

D1434466

Lang**Syne**
PUBLISHING
WRITING *to* REMEMBER

Lang**Syne**

PUBLISHING

WRITING *to* REMEMBER

Strathclyde Business Centre
120 Carstairs Street, Glasgow G40 4JD
Tel: 0141 554 9944 Fax: 0141 554 9955
E-mail: info@scottish-memories.co.uk
www.langsyneshop.co.uk

Design by Dorothy Meikle
Printed by Thomson Litho, East Kilbride
© Lang Syne Publishers Ltd 2008

ISBN 1-85217-274-6

Ryan

MOTTO:
I would rather die than be dishonoured.

CREST:
A griffin holding a sword.

NAME variations include:
Ó Maolriain *(Gaelic)*,
Ó Maoilriaghain *(Gaelic)*,
Mulrian, O'Mulryan,
O'Ryan, O'Riain.

Chapter one:
Origins of Irish surnames

**According to an old saying, there are two types of Irish –
those who actually are Irish and those who wish they were.**

This sentiment is only one example of the allure that the
high romance and drama of the proud nation's history holds
for thousands of people scattered across the world today.

It's a sad fact, however, that the vast majority of Irish
surnames are found far beyond Irish shores, rather than on
the Emerald Isle itself.

The population stood at around eight million souls in
1841, but today it stands at fewer than six million.

This is mainly a tragic consequence of the potato
famine, also known as the Great Hunger, which devastated
Ireland between 1845 and 1849.

The Irish peasantry had become almost wholly reliant
for basic sustenance on the potato, first introduced from the
Americas in the seventeenth century.

When the crop was hit by a blight, at least 800,000
people starved to death while an estimated two million
others were forced to seek a new life far from their native
shores – particularly in America, Canada, and Australia.

The effects of the potato blight continued until about
1851, by which time a firm pattern of emigration had
become established.

Ireland's loss, however, was to the gain of the countries in which the immigrants settled, contributing enormously, as their descendants do today, to the well being of the nations in which their forefathers settled.

But those who were forced through dire circumstance to establish a new life in foreign parts never forgot their roots, or the proud heritage and traditions of the land that gave them birth.

Nor do their descendants.

It is a heritage that is inextricably bound up in the colourful variety of Irish names themselves – and the origin and history of these names forms an integral part of the vibrant drama that is the nation's history, one of both glorious fortune and tragic misfortune.

This history is well documented, and one of the most important and fascinating of the earliest sources are *The Annals of the Four Masters*, compiled between 1632 and 1636 by four friars at the Franciscan Monastery in County Donegal.

Compiled from earlier sources, and purporting to go back to the Biblical Deluge, much of the material takes in the mythological origins and history of Ireland and the Irish.

This includes tales of successive waves of invaders and settlers such as the Fomorians, the Partholonians, the Nemedians, the Fir Bolgs, the Tuatha De Danann, and the Laigain.

Of particular interest are the *Milesian Genealogies*,

because the majority of Irish clans today claim a descent from either Heremon, Ir, or Heber – three of the sons of Milesius, a king of what is now modern day Spain.

These sons invaded Ireland in the second millennium B.C, apparently in fulfilment of a mysterious prophecy received by their father.

This Milesian lineage is said to have ruled Ireland for nearly 3,000 years, until the island came under the sway of England's King Henry II in 1171 following what is known as the Cambro-Norman invasion.

This is an important date not only in Irish history in general, but for the effect the invasion subsequently had for Irish surnames.

'Cambro' comes from the Welsh, and 'Cambro-Norman' describes those Welsh knights of Norman origin who invaded Ireland.

But they were invaders who stayed, inter-marrying with the native Irish population and founding their own proud dynasties that bore Cambro-Norman names such as Archer, Barbour, Brannagh, Fitzgerald, Fitzgibbon, Fleming, Joyce, Plunkett, and Walsh – to name only a few.

These 'Cambro-Norman' surnames that still flourish throughout the world today form one of the three main categories in which Irish names can be placed – those of Gaelic-Irish, Cambro-Norman, and Anglo-Irish.

Previous to the Cambro-Norman invasion of the twelfth century, and throughout the earlier invasions and settlement of those wild bands of sea rovers known as the Vikings in the eighth and ninth centuries, the population of the island was relatively small, and it was normal for a person to be identified through the use of only a forename.

But as population gradually increased and there were many more people with the same forename, surnames were adopted to distinguish one person, or one community, from another.

Individuals identified themselves with their own particular tribe, or 'tuath', and this tribe – that also became known as a clann, or clan – took its name from some distinguished ancestor who had founded the clan.

The Gaelic-Irish form of the name Kelly, for example, is Ó Ceallaigh, or O'Kelly, indicating descent from an original 'Ceallaigh', with the 'O' denoting 'grandson of.' The name was later anglicised to Kelly.

The prefix 'Mac' or 'Mc', meanwhile, as with the clans of the Scottish Highlands, denotes 'son of.'

Although the Irish clans had much in common with their Scottish counterparts, one important difference lies in what are known as 'septs', or branches, of the clan.

Septs of Scottish clans were groups who often bore an entirely different name from the clan name but were under the clan's protection.

In Ireland, septs were groups that shared the same name and who could be found scattered throughout the four provinces of Ulster, Leinster, Munster, and Connacht.

The 'golden age' of the Gaelic-Irish clans, infused as their veins were with the blood of Celts, pre-dates the Viking invasions of the eighth and ninth centuries and the Norman invasion of the twelfth century, and the sacred heart of the country was the Hill of Tara, near the River Boyne, in County Meath.

Known in Gaelic as 'Teamhar na Rí', or Hill of Kings, it was the royal seat of the 'Ard Rí Éireann', or High King of Ireland, to whom the petty kings, or chieftains, from the island's provinces were ultimately subordinate.

It was on the Hill of Tara, beside a stone pillar known as the Irish 'Lia Fáil', or Stone of Destiny, that the High Kings were inaugurated and, according to legend, this stone would emit a piercing screech that could be heard all over Ireland when touched by the hand of the rightful king.

The Hill of Tara is today one of the island's main tourist attractions.

Opposition to English rule over Ireland, established in the wake of the Cambro-Norman invasion, broke out frequently and the harsh solution adopted by the powerful forces of the Crown was to forcibly evict the native Irish from their lands.

These lands were then granted to Protestant colonists, or 'planters', from Britain.

Many of these colonists, ironically, came from Scotland and were the descendants of the original 'Scotti', or 'Scots', who gave their name to Scotland after migrating there in the fifth century A.D., from the north of Ireland.

Colonisation entailed harsh penal laws being imposed on the majority of the native Irish population, stripping them practically of all of their rights.

The Crown's main bastion in Ireland was Dublin and its environs, known as the Pale, and it was the dispossessed peasantry who lived outside this Pale, desperately striving to eke out a meagre living.

It was this that gave rise to the modern-day expression of someone or something being 'beyond the pale'.

Attempts were made to stamp out all aspects of the ancient Gaelic-Irish culture, to the extent that even to bear a Gaelic-Irish name was to invite discrimination.

This is why many Gaelic-Irish names were anglicised with, for example, and noted above, Ó Ceallaigh, or O'Kelly, being anglicised to Kelly.

Succeeding centuries have seen strong revivals of Gaelic-Irish consciousness, however, and this has led to many families reverting back to the original form of their name, while the language itself is frequently found on the fluent tongues of an estimated 90,000 to 145,000 of the island's population.

Ireland's turbulent history of religious and political strife is one that lasted well into the twentieth century, a landmark century that saw the partition of the island into the twenty-six counties of the independent Republic of

Ireland, or Eire, and the six counties of Northern Ireland, or Ulster.

Dublin, originally founded by Vikings, is now a vibrant and truly cosmopolitan city while the proud city of Belfast is one of the jewels in the crown of Ulster.

It was Saint Patrick who first brought the light of Christianity to Ireland in the fifth century A.D.

Interpretations of this Christian message have varied over the centuries, often leading to bitter sectarian conflict – but the many intricately sculpted Celtic Crosses found all over the island are symbolic of a unity that crosses the sectarian divide.

It is an image that fuses the 'old gods' of the Celts with Christianity.

All the signs from the early years of this new millennium indicate that sectarian strife may soon become a thing of the past – with the Irish and their many kinsfolk across the world, be they Protestant or Catholic, finding common purpose in the rich tapestry of their shared heritage.

Chapter two:

The little kings

**While there are various theories concerning the origins
of the name of Ryan and while distinct septs, or branches,
of the family flourished in different geographical
locations throughout Ireland, what bearers of the
surname had in common for centuries was a fierce
resolve to defend their ancient rights in the face of
aggression.**

As a native Irish clan, the Ryans have a long and
colourful pedigree – one that stretches so far back through
the mists of time that historical fact becomes enmeshed in
myth and legend.

In common with other native Irish clans, the Ryans
trace a descent from one of the sons of Milesius, a king of
what is now modern day Spain, and who had planned to
invade Ireland in fulfilment of a mysterious Druidic
prophecy.

Milesius died before he could launch his invasion across
the sea to Ireland, but eight sons who included Amergin,
Hebor, Ir, and Heremon undertook the task.

Five sons, including Ir, were killed in battle against the
Tuatha-De-Danann shortly after battling their way from the
shoreline to the soil of Ireland.

This was soil, however, that Ir's offspring and the

offspring of his brothers Heber and Heremon were destined to hold for centuries as warrior kings.

According to the Milesian genealogies, Heremon and Heber began to rule the land they had conquered from about 1699 B.C.

The Ryans trace a descent back to Heremon, who killed both Amergin and Heber in quarrels over territory.

Boasting a descent from these ancient kings of Ireland may explain why the name 'Ryan' is held to signify 'little king' – stemming from the Gaelic 'righ', meaning 'king', and 'an' signifying 'little'.

Ryan' is the modern anglicised version of the original Irish Gaelic 'Ó Maoilriain', or 'O' Riain', while some sources assert the name stems from 'O'Maoilriaghan', indicating 'descendant or devotee of St. Riaghan.'

'Maol', 'Maoil', or 'Mul', is held to indicate 'bald'.

Whatever the origins of the name, most septs of the family claim a descent, originating through Heremon, with the early second century A.D. Irish king Cathair Mór.

One of Cathair Mór's descendants was Drona, founder of the Ui Drona, or Idrone, whose territory lay in present day Carlow and Kilkenny.

The early presence of these Lords of Idrone can still be seen on the Irish landscape – most notably in the form of the Abbey of Duiske, near Graiguenamanagh, built on land granted to the Cistercian Order in the late twelfth century by the powerful Dermot O'Ryan of Idrone.

Ryans also flourished in what was known as the barony of Owney, on the borders of Limerick and Tipperary.

With the benefit of a great deal of historical hindsight, it is accurate to say that what would prove to be the death knell of many proud native Irish clans such as the Ryans was sounded in the late twelfth century.

Twelfth century Ireland was far from being a unified nation, split up as it was into territories ruled over by squabbling chieftains such as those of the Ryans – and this inter-clan rivalry and disunity worked to the advantage of invaders.

In a series of bloody conflicts one chieftain, or king, would occasionally gain the upper hand over his rivals, and by 1156 the most powerful was Muirchertach MacLochlainn, king of the powerful O'Neills.

He was opposed by the equally powerful Rory O'Connor, king of the province of Connacht, but he increased his power and influence by allying himself with Dermot MacMurrough, king of Leinster.

MacLochlainn and MacMurrough were aware that the main key to the kingdom of Ireland was the thriving trading port of Dublin that had been established by invading Vikings, or Ostmen, in 852 A.D.

The port was taken by the combined forces of the Leinster and Connacht kings, but when MacLochlainn died the Dubliners rose up in revolt and overthrew the unpopular MacMurrough.

A triumphant Rory O'Connor entered Dublin and was later inaugurated as Ard Rí, but MacMurrough was not one to humbly accept defeat.

He appealed for help from England's Henry II in unseating O'Connor, an act that was to radically affect the future course of Ireland's fortunes.

The English monarch agreed to help MacMurrough, but distanced himself from direct action by delegating his Norman subjects in Wales with the task.

These ambitious and battle-hardened barons and knights had first settled in Wales following the Norman Conquest of England in 1066 and, with an eye on rich booty, plunder, and lands, were only too eager to obey their sovereign's wishes and furnish MacMurrough with aid.

He crossed the Irish Sea to Bristol, where he rallied powerful barons such as Robert Fitzstephen and Maurice Fitzgerald to his cause, along with Gilbert de Clare, Earl of Pembroke, also known as Strongbow.

A mighty Norman invasion force was assembled in Wales and crossed the sea to Ireland.

Their onslaught on the forces of Rory O'Connor and his allies was so disciplined and fierce that by 1171 they had re-captured Dublin, in the name of MacMurrough, and other strategically important territories.

It was now that a nervous Henry II began to take cold feet over the venture, realising that he may have created a rival in the form of a separate Norman kingdom in Ireland.

Accordingly, he landed on the island, near Waterford, at the head of a large army in October of 1171 with the aim of curbing the power of his Cambro-Norman barons.

Protracted war between the king and his barons was averted, however, when they submitted to the royal will, promising homage and allegiance in return for holding the territories they had conquered in the king's name.

Henry also received the submission and homage of many of the Irish chieftains, tired as they were with internecine warfare and also perhaps realising that as long as they were rivals and not united they were no match for the powerful forces the English Crown could muster.

English dominion over Ireland was ratified through the Treaty of Windsor of 1175, while successive waves of English settlers followed in the wake of the Cambro-Norman barons.

Through time there were actually three separate and distinct 'Irelands.'

There were the territories of the privileged and powerful Norman barons and their retainers, the Ireland of the disaffected Gaelic-Irish such as the Ryans who held lands unoccupied by the Normans, and the Pale – comprised of Dublin itself and a substantial area of its environs ruled over by an English elite.

Descendants of many of the original Norman barons, such as the Fitzgeralds, assimilated to such an extent with the native Irish culture that they have been described as having become 'more Irish than the Irish.'

What united them with many native Irish families such as the Ryans was their opposition to the growing dominance in their affairs of the English Crown – in particular a policy of 'planting' loyal Protestants on land held by Catholics.

This policy had started during the reign from 1491 to 1547 of Henry VIII, whose Reformation effectively outlawed the established Roman Catholic faith of families such as the Ryans throughout his dominions.

The Ryans found themselves frequently in alliance with families such as the Fitzgeralds in resisting the encroachment on their territories of waves of settlers, a resistance that took the form of violent rebellion and insurrection.

Chapter three:

Rebellion and exile

The practice of settling Protestants in Ireland, combined with attempts to stamp the Crown's authority on the island continued under the reign of Elizabeth, the bastard daughter of Henry VIII, culminating in an attempt to curb the power of feudal lords such as the Fitzgeralds by appointing Crown commissioners to their territories and effectively de-militarising them.

With the Fitzgerald Earl of Desmond and his two brothers held in the grim confines of the Tower of London following their defeat against the Butler Earl of Ormonde at the battle of Affane in 1565, leadership of the Fitzgeralds in Munster fell to James Fitzmaurice Fitzgerald, described as 'captain general' of the powerful family.

Resolving to curb the encroachments of the Crown on the Fitzgerald territory and to strike a blow into the bargain against the rival Earl of Ormonde, Fitzmaurice effectively declared war on the Crown when, supported by native Irish clans such as the MacCarthys, O'Sullivans, O'Keefes, and Ryans, he descended on an English colony south of Cork in June of 1569.

Cork city was then attacked, followed by a siege of the Earl of Ormonde's stronghold of Kilkenny the following month.

Fitzmaurice had cleverly exploited divisions in the

Butler Earl of Ormonde's family by enlisting the support of two of his brothers while the Earl was in London; he soon returned, however, and swung his family around in support of the Crown.

Henry Sidney, Lord Deputy of Ireland, reacted to the sudden insurrection by mobilising troops in the island itself and enlisting the aid of more troops rapidly despatched to meet the emergency from England.

Sidney appointed Humphrey Gilbert as governor of Munster, and under his direction the province was devastated and hundreds of innocent civilians summarily put to the sword.

As Munster groaned under this terror and became a virtual wasteland, Fitzmaurice and his allies such as the Ryans resorted to daring guerrilla tactics launched from their base in the Kerry mountains, but they were no match for the superior might of the Crown.

Many of Fitzmaurice's allies were forced into surrender, and in February of 1573 Fitzmaurice himself surrendered after promise of a pardon.

What has become known as The First Desmond Rebellion had been quashed, with Fitzmaurice leaving for France in 1575, but the embers of rebellion were still there – only awaiting the spark that launched the Second Desmond Rebellion.

James Fitzmaurice Fitzgerald returned from his exile on the continent in 1579.

He had certainly not been idle during his four years of exile; as a devout Roman Catholic he had enlisted the aid of no less than the Pope and King Phillip II of Spain in what became a crusade to crush the power of the English Crown once and for all in Ireland.

Cornelius O'Mulryan, the Franciscan Bishop of Cloyne and Ross and also Bishop of Killala, and a brother of the Ryan chief of Owney, played a crucial role in the negotiations with the Papacy and the Spanish monarch.

This culminated in Fitzgerald, along with the Pope's blessing, troops, and money, in addition to a number of Spanish and Italian troops, landing at Smerwick, in Co. Kerry, on July 18 of 1579, intent on the invasion of Munster.

The Earl of Desmond and his brothers had earlier been released from their captivity in the Tower of London and one of these brothers, John Fitzgerald, rallied to his kinsman Fitzmaurice's desperate cause.

The rebellion would have been left leaderless had John Fitzgerald not joined the rebels, because Fitzmaurice was killed in a skirmish only a few weeks later.

John Fitzgerald assumed the leadership, but his brother, the Earl of Desmond, rather reluctantly assumed this mantle a short time later after the Crown declared him a traitor.

The rebels struck a number of stunning blows against the Crown under the Earl's leadership, including the sacking of the towns of Youghal and Kinsale, but by the summer of

1580 they were mainly on the defensive, despite the rebellion having spread into Leinster.

Reinforcements to the rebel cause arrived in September of 1580 in the form of troops despatched by the Pope; but they surrendered and were massacred to the last man only a short time after they landed in Kerry after being besieged in a fort at Dun an Oir.

The rebellion dragged on, however, only reaching an exhausted conclusion in November of 1583 when the Earl of Desmond was killed near Tralee, in Kerry.

Cornelius O'Mulryan was one of the many rebels who had to flee in to exile, dying in Spain in 1617.

The settlement of loyal Protestants in Ireland continued throughout the subsequent reign of James I (James VI of Scotland.

In an insurrection that exploded in 1641, at least 2,000 Protestant settlers were massacred at the hands of Catholic landowners and their native Irish peasantry, while thousands more were stripped of their belongings and driven from their lands to seek refuge where they could.

Terrible as the atrocities were against the Protestant settlers, subsequent accounts became greatly exaggerated, serving to fuel a burning desire on the part of Protestants for revenge against the rebels.

Tragically for Ireland, this revenge became directed not only against the rebels, but native Irish Catholics such as the Ryans in general.

The English Civil War intervened to prevent immediate action against the rebels, but following the execution of Charles I in 1649 and the consolidation of the power of England's fanatically Protestant Oliver Cromwell, the time was ripe for revenge.

The Lord Protector, as he was named, descended on Ireland at the head of a 20,000-strong army that landed at Ringford, near Dublin, in August of 1649.

The consequences of this Cromwellian conquest still resonate throughout the island today.

Cromwell had three main aims: to quash all forms of rebellion, to 'remove' all Catholic landowners who had taken part in the rebellion, and to convert the native Irish to the Protestant faith.

An early warning of the terrors that were in store for the native Catholic Irish came when the northeastern town of Drogheda was stormed and taken in September and between 2,000 and 4,000 of its inhabitants killed, including priests who were summarily put to the sword.

The defenders of Drogheda's St. Peter's Church were burned to death as they huddled for refuge in the steeple and the church was deliberately torched.

In Wexford, on the southeast coast, at least 1,500 of its inhabitants were slaughtered, including 200 defenceless women, despite their pathetic pleas for mercy.

Three hundred other inhabitants of the town drowned when their overladen boats sank as they desperately tried to flee to safety, while a group of Franciscan friars were massacred in their church.

Cromwell soon held Ireland in a grip of iron, allowing him to implement what amounted to a policy of ethnic cleansing.

His troopers were given free rein to hunt down and kill priests, while all Catholic estates, such as those of the Ryans, were systematically confiscated.

Native Irish families such as the Ryans enjoyed a brief resurgence in their fortunes following the Restoration of Charles II in 1660.

But these fortunes went into final and fatal decline following the 'Glorious Revolution' of 1688 that saw the flight into exile of James II (James VII of Scotland) and the accession to the throne of the Protestant Prince William of Orange and his wife, Mary.

Adherents of the Catholic monarch James were known as Jacobites, and among those Jacobites who fought for his cause were a number of Ryans.

The Jacobite forces were defeated at the battle of the Boyne in July of 1690, with final defeat recognised and ratified through the signing of the Treaty of Limerick in October of the following year.

Under the terms of the treaty, many Jacobite officers were allowed to seek exile in France and Spain, where they fought bravely for the cause of their adopted nations.

Chapter four:

On the world stage

Generations of Ryans have dominated, and continue to dominate, a range of pursuits – not least the world of entertainment.

An actress who specialises in romantic comedies, Margaret Hyra took her mother's maiden name of Ryan and is better known as **Meg Ryan**.

Born in Fairfield, Connecticut, in 1961, she has appeared in a number of films, most notably the 1986 *Top Gun*, the 1989 *When Harry Met Sally*, and the 1993 *Sleepless in Seattle*.

Born in Chicago in 1909, **Robert Ryan** was the actor who had a number of jobs, including ship's stoker, rancher, and labourer, before turning his talents to acting.

A school boxing champion, he was well suited for his role in the 1940 movie *Golden Gloves*, while other films include *Crossfire* (1947), *Flying Leathernecks* (1951), *The Dirty Dozen* (1967), and *Executive Action*, filmed before his death in 1973.

Best known for her role as Xena in the 1995 to 2001 television series *Xena: Warrior Princess*, **Lucy Lawless** is the actress who was born Lucille Frances Ryan in Mount Albert, New Zealand, in 1968, while several centuries earlier **Lacy Ryan**, born in 1694, was an acclaimed English actor who appeared on stage in London's famous Haymarket and Covent Garden theatres.

The daughter of an American mother and an Irish father, Irene Noblette, born in El Paso, Texas, in 1902 and who died in 1973, was better known as the Emmy and Tony Award-nominated actress **Irene Ryan**, who achieved fame not only in television and film, but earlier in vaudeville, radio and on the Broadway stage.

She is best known for her role as 'Granny' in the television series *The Beverley Hillbillies* that ran from 1962 to 1971. Her first husband was the actor **Tom Ryan**.

Born in Boston in 1967, **Blanchard Ryan** is the American actress who has starred in films such as the 2004 *Open Water*, while **Peggy Ryan**, born in Long Beach California and who died in 2004 was the dancer who first appeared on stage in vaudeville with her parents as part of 'The Merry Dancing Ryans.'

She starred in a number of movie musicals, including the 1937 *Top of the Town* and the 1942 *When Johnny Comes Marching Home*.

'Ryans' also feature in two famous films, in the form of the 1970 *Ryan's Daughter*, set in Ireland and which starred John Mills, Robert Mitchum, and Sara Miles, and Steven Spielberg's *Saving Private Ryan*, from 1998, starring Tom Hanks.

Bianca Ryan, born in Philadelphia in 1994, is the talented young American singer of both Irish and Japanese ancestry who won the debut season of the *America's Got Talent* show at the tender age of eleven, while **Gerry Ryan**, born in Dublin in 1956, is one of Ireland's most popular radio presenters.

In the highly competitive world of sport, **Bo Ryan**, born in Pennsylvania in 1947, is a leading American basketball coach, while **Bob Ryan**, born in Trenton, New Jersey, in 1947 is the *Boston Globe* columnist described as a basketball 'guru', because of his incisive coverage of the sport.

From basketball to baseball, **Nolan Ryan**, born in Refugic, Texas, in 1947, is recognised at the time of writing as the sport's all-time leader in strikeouts. The right-handed pitcher was inducted into the Baseball Hall of Fame in 1999.

Nicknamed 'Pony', **Jimmy Ryan**, who was born in Clinton, Massachusetts, in 1863 was the American centre midfielder who played Major League Baseball for a number of Chicago teams in the National League, while **B.J. Ryan**, born in 1975 in Bossier City, Louisiana, is a Major League baseball closer at the time of writing for the Toronto Blue Jays of the American League.

In the world of athletics, **Patrick J. Ryan** was the Olympic hammer-throwing champion who was born in Co. Limerick, Ireland, in 1883 and who immigrated to America in 1901 and joined the New York Police Department.

His world record throw of 189ft, set in 1913, was not beaten until 24 years later.

In contemporary times, **Kevin Ryan**, born in Auckland, New Zealand, in 1948, is the former long-distance runner who represented his nation in the 1976 Summer Olympics, while **Prestin Ryan**, born in 1980, is the Canadian ice hockey player who at the time of writing plays for the Vancouver Canucks organisation.

Born in Sharon, Ontario, in 1983, **Matt Ryan** is another noted ice hockey player who, at the time of writing, plays for the Los Angeles Kings.

In the bruising world of boxing, **Tommy Ryan**, born in Redwood, New York, in 1870, was a famous welterweight and middleweight champion, while on the rugby pitch **Andrew Ryan**, born in Dubbo, New South Wales, in 1978, is the Australian professional rugby league player, nicknamed 'Bobcat' who, at the time of writing, is captain of the Canterbury Bulldogs.

Ryans have also been prominent in the world of American football – including the former leading coach **Buddy Ryan**, who was born in Frederick, Oklahoma, in 1934, while **Frank Ryan**, born in Texas in 1936, is the retired quarterback who played for teams including the Washington Redskins, the Cleveland Browns, and the Los Angeles Rams.

Greg Ryan, born in Dallas in 1957 is at the time of writing, head coach of the United States women's national soccer team.

On the field of battle, no less than four Ryans – three of

them sharing the forename John – were recipients of the Victoria Cross (V.C.), the highest award for gallantry for British and Commonwealth forces.

Born in Kilkenny, Ireland, in 1823, **John Ryan** was a private in the 1st Madras Fusiliers, Indian Army, during the Indian Mutiny.

He was awarded the V.C. for his bravery in rescuing wounded comrades at Lucknow in September of 1857; he survived this action only to be killed in action less than a year later.

Another Irish soldier, **John Ryan**, born in Barnsleigh, Co. Tipperary in 1839, was a Lance Corporal in the 65th Regiment of Foot, British Army, during the Waikato-Hauhau Maori War in New Zealand, in 1863.

He was awarded his V.C. after helping to remove the body of his mortally wounded captain from the field of action – only to be drowned two months later while trying to rescue a comrade.

Born in Australia in 1890, **John Ryan** was a private in the 55th Battalion (New South Wales) Australian Imperial Force during the First World War. He won his V.C. in September of 1918 at the Hindenburg Defences, in France, after organising and leading a party of men against the enemy.

He died in 1941.

Miles Ryan, born in Derry in 1826, was another Irishman who won a V.C. during the Indian Mutiny.

A drummer in the 1st Battalion European Bengal Fusiliers, he and his sergeant had saved their comrades' lives in September of 1857 by throwing burning boxes of ammunition that threatened to explode in their faces over part of the defensive ramparts of Delhi.

He died in 1887.

Also on the field of battle, **Chris Ryan**, born in 1961, is the British soldier and former member of the elite Special Air Squadron (S.A.S.), who managed to escape against all the odds from Iraq into Syria during the first Gulf War when his patrol came under attack.

Travelling over 200 miles on foot in seven days he was later awarded the Military Medal. He is now a successful author. Born in Dublin in 1920, **Cornelius Ryan**, who died in 1974, was the Irish journalist and author whose many books on popular military history include *The Longest Day*, concerning the D-Day invasion of Normandy in 1944 and *A Bridge Too Far*, concerning the assault by airborne forces on the Netherlands before the battle of Arnhem. Both novels became the basis of successful films of the same name.

Although he is thought to have been the basis for the character of Liam Devlin in the 1975 Jack Higgins novel *The Eagle has Landed*, also a successful film, there was nothing fictitious about the hair-raising life and times of **Frank Ryan**, born in Elton, Co. Limerick, in 1902.

A prominent member at one stage of the Irish Republican Army and leader of the Irish Volunteers during the Spanish

Civil War, he fought against British interests during the Second World War by working on behalf of German military intelligence.

He died and was buried in Germany in 1944, but his body was re-interred in Dublin's Glasnevin Cemetery in 1979.

In the world of politics, **Thomas Joseph Ryan**, born in 1876, was Premier of Queensland, Australia, from 1915 to 1919, while **Patricia Ryan Nixon**, born Thelma Catherine Ryan in Ely, Nevada, in 1912 and who died in 1993, was First Lady of the United States from 1969 to 1974 as the wife of President Richard Nixon.

Taking to the skies, Ryanair, the third largest airline in Europe, was founded in 1985 by entrepreneurs that included Irishmen **Christy Ryan** and **Tony Ryan**.

While generations of Ryans made the long journey by sea across the Atlantic to seek a new life, it was **Claude T. Ryan** who designed the first aeroplane to fly a man successfully across the vast ocean – the famous *Spirit of St. Louis*, flown by the intrepid aviator Charles Lindbergh in 1927.

Key dates in Ireland's history from the first settlers to the formation of the Irish Republic:

circa 7000 B.C.	Arrival and settlement of Stone Age people.
circa 3000 B.C.	Arrival of settlers of New Stone Age period.
circa 600 B.C.	First arrival of the Celts.
200 A.D.	Establishment of Hill of Tara, Co. Meath, as seat of the High Kings.
circa 432 A.D.	Christian mission of St. Patrick.
800-920 A.D.	Invasion and subsequent settlement of Vikings.
1002 A.D.	Brian Boru recognised as High King.
1014	Brian Boru killed at battle of Clontarf.
1169-1170	Cambro-Norman invasion of the island.
1171	Henry II claims Ireland for the English Crown.
1366	Statutes of Kilkenny ban marriage between native Irish and English.
1529-1536	England's Henry VIII embarks on religious Reformation.
1536	Earl of Kildare rebels against the Crown.
1541	Henry VIII declared King of Ireland.
1558	Accession to English throne of Elizabeth I.
1565	Battle of Affane.
1569-1573	First Desmond Rebellion.
1579-1583	Second Desmond Rebellion.
1594-1603	Nine Years War.
1606	Plantation' of Scottish and English settlers.
1607	Flight of the Earls.
1632-1636	Annals of the Four Masters compiled.
1641	Rebellion over policy of plantation and other grievances.
1649	Beginning of Cromwellian conquest.
1688	Flight into exile in France of Catholic Stuart monarch James II as Protestant Prince William of Orange invited to take throne of England along with his wife, Mary.
1689	William and Mary enthroned as joint monarchs; siege of Derry.
1690	Jacobite forces of James defeated by William at battle of the Boyne (July) and Dublin taken.

1691	Athlone taken by William; Jacobite defeats follow at Aughrim, Galway, and Limerick; conflict ends with Treaty of Limerick (October) and Irish officers allowed to leave for France.
1695	Penal laws introduced to restrict rights of Catholics; banishment of Catholic clergy.
1704	Laws introduced constricting rights of Catholics in landholding and public office.
1728	Franchise removed from Catholics.
1791	Foundation of United Irishmen republican movement.
1796	French invasion force lands in Bantry Bay.
1798	Defeat of Rising in Wexford and death of United Irishmen leaders Wolfe Tone and Lord Edward Fitzgerald.
1800	Act of Union between England and Ireland.
1803	Dublin Rising under Robert Emmet.
1829	Catholics allowed to sit in Parliament.
1845-1849	The Great Hunger: thousands starve to death as potato crop fails and thousands more emigrate.
1856	Phoenix Society founded.
1858	Irish Republican Brotherhood established.
1873	Foundation of Home Rule League.
1893	Foundation of Gaelic League.
1904	Foundation of Irish Reform Association.
1913	Dublin strikes and lockout.
1916	Easter Rising in Dublin and proclamation of an Irish Republic.
1917	Irish Parliament formed after Sinn Fein election victory.
1919-1921	War between Irish Republican Army and British Army.
1922	Irish Free State founded, while six northern counties remain part of United Kingdom as Northern Ireland, or Ulster; civil war up until 1923 between rival republican groups.
1949	Foundation of Irish Republic after all remaining constitutional links with Britain are severed.